PRAISE FOR WE
I Should Have Lif

"What a beautiful title. I
the heart of what it mean
we should and ought t
other. Instead we are only human beings who uo as we
as we can, but don't quite manage all the same. . . . I
think that many readers will recognise themselves and
take pleasure in reading this book, whether you are in
this very situation or have been there. The text has an
energy that feels real and strong. The same applies to the
language, which is compact and beautiful. This is a
book that moves you. It puts powerfully into words the
complex emotions of the process of sorrow."

Siri M Kvamme, *Bergens Tidende*, Norway

"The book is based on Mühleisen's thoughts, memories
and reflections, written in the style of a diary after her
mother Ellen Sofie Rolstorph Fugelli died of cancer in
2006, aged 85. She was married to a man who fought
on the German side during the war. She became the
mother of four children, and was generally so taken up
with looking after house and home that she had no time
to build a separate identity or become involved in great
political questions. Mühleisen is, in contrast, a feminist,
left-wing radical, performance artist, gender and media
researcher. This is therefore the story of two generations
of women, strangers to each other's life, where the
younger has to look after her mother on her deathbed,
and afterwards feels a great sorrow."

Miriam Lund Knapstad, *Aftenposten*, Norway

"The relationship between mother and daughter is central. Unlike the relationship with fathers, the relationship with mothers is more tinged with feelings of guilt, is more diffuse and problematic, disappearing without trace into different private spaces. It is hardly something to build on, more often something to run away from, to forget. Mühleisen treats the theme with a kind of singing, humming ambivalence; the emotions that are expressed are both bitter and angry, warm and loving. Especially at the beginning of the novel, the tone is unremitting and raw."

Susanne Christensen, *Klassekampen*, Norway

"The fact that Mühleisen continually reflects on her relationship with her mother enriches the story that, simply stated, deals with death and life. For Mühleisen strives all the time to find a common anchoring point for herself and her mother. Some kind of lowest common denominator. By rattling off what her mother has done and is doing, Mühleisen highlights the contrasts between the generations. What they have in common is that they love each other. They are women from two generations with enormous differences, and Mühleisen brings the differences to account. . . . A fine, intimate story."

Mina Th. Watz, *Oppland Arbeiderblad*, Norway

"This is not a heroising and unambiguous portrait she paints of her mother. At the same time, her mother's death loosens an avalanche of tenderness, which among other things finds expression in a last wish to turn back time in order to make her passage easier, like a caring mother – *"then I just take you into my embrace and lift you carefully over."*

Kari Løvaas, *Morgenbladet*, Norway

WENCKE MÜHLEISEN

Born 1953 to a Norwegian mother and Slovenian-Austrian father, Wencke Mühleisen is a writer and academic in media, gender and sexuality studies at the University of Stavanger. From 1978–1989, she was active as a performance artist dealing with issues such as gender, sexuality, feminism and politics and she lived in a radical artists' collective in Austria from 1976–1985.

I Should Have Lifted You Carefully Over is her first novel, published to critical acclaim in Norway.

Located on the Isle of Arran in Scotland, Anne Bruce formerly worked in education and has a longstanding love of Scandinavia and Norway in particular. She studied Norwegian and English at Glasgow University, covering both nynorsk and bokmål language and literature, as well as Old Norse, Icelandic, Swedish and Danish. She has travelled extensively in Scandinavia and under-taken translation and interpretation work, recently translating two contemporary novels.

I SHOULD HAVE LIFTED YOU CAREFULLY OVER

Recordings

WENCKE MÜHLEISEN

Translated from the Norwegian by Anne Bruce

SANDSTONEPRESS
HIGHLAND | SCOTLAND

First published in Great Britain 2011
Sandstone Press Ltd
PO Box 5725
One High Street
Dingwall
Ross-shire
IV15 9WJ

www.sandstonepress.com

English Language Editor: Robert Davidson

This translation has been published with the financial support of NORLA.

The publisher acknowledges subsidy from
Creative Scotland towards publication of this volume.

ISBN: 978-1-905207- 64-0

Sandstone Press is committed to a sustainable future in publishing, marrying
the needs of the company and our readers with those of the wider envir-
onment. This book is made from paper certified by the Forest Stewardship
Council.

Cover by River Design, Edinburgh, from an original design by
Blaest Design, Oslo, Norway
Typeset by Iolaire Typesetting, Newtonmore.
Printed and bound in Poland.

For Mercedes and Isis and for Sidsel, Brit and Erik

I always think about the people who build buildings when they are not around any more. Or a movie with a crowd scene and everybody's dead. It's frightening.

ANDY WARHOL

CONTENTS

OPENING SHOT

You are lying on your side just the way you fell asleep. Your eyes are not closed. Your condition before you took your last forceful breaths can't have been sleep. You were suffocating before you died. This is the last position you unwillingly folded yourself into before the force of gravity finally overcame you on your widow's bed. I stare at you after these three days and nights of hard dying. You and I together, Mum. You and I. I can't touch you. Death is flat and solid. The stink of death and excrement hang thick and silent in the air around me. It's over. Clever girl. Mum. Mother superior. *Mutter-mörder?*

If I don't look out for myself now, Mum, if I don't take great care, the sorrow for you will harden forever. Either: Oh, you, my demon mother! Or: Oh, you, my lovely mother! My dead object. I swallow you up. I immerse you deep in the poisonous and preserving juices of my guts. A last snapshot. Freeze frame. Death mask. Empty grimace. In the chapel before they burn this to ashes. This is deadly serious: a perilous, lasting and life-giving connection. I won't let you burn in hell. I won't kneel before your beautiful picture. No stiffening up. Cross my heart!

– I found out today that I have cancer, Mum said on the telephone in January from the hospital in Kristiansand. My blood thickens. Pulsing through the veins. I am pressed down on the office chair. I stare at the wall in front of me. Photographs of my two daughters. – A big tumour on my lung. And one on my liver. I have to go to a meeting in five minutes. Three to six months, maybe, she says. Like a long holiday, I think. Last holiday.

On Tuesday the doctor rang me about chemotherapy and other treatment. There is certainly no point in chemotherapy. She is too old. Too weak. She would die of the side effects. It is perhaps something you have to expect when you get old. To die of cancer. Of course she has smoked since she was young. Mum seems relieved when I speak to her on the phone. All the same, she is afraid of pain and perhaps of not having as much time as she hopes. She seems almost content.

– I don't think I'm worried about dying, she says. Just strange to think that I won't be able to be with you children any longer. I hope I don't get pains at the end.

It was quiet.

– It'll soon be spring, and I'll see the sky over Jæren again, she says suddenly. As if optimistic. Expectant. I feel sick. What pathetic resignation! Is she being considerate? I want to scream down the telephone. Scold her. This sickly devotion. This dull, self-besotted suffering. Does she think there's something wonderful about it? I say that I'll phone back later.

– Look, how soft my hands have become, she says to the six-year-old child who stands beside her bed. Me. In my parents' bedroom. The newborn baby – my sister – in a woven laundry basket beside us. Soft hands? Why does Mum have such soft hands? I stroke them gingerly. Soft. But why? – Why do you have such soft hands, Mum? – It's because I've been in the maternity unit all week, and haven't had my hands in water, like I always do when I'm washing up, washing clothes, and cleaning. They get rough, cracked and split open.

Will I stand there again now? Beside your bed. Sick bed. Stand there! Like, just stand there. Witness your suffering. Just listen to you saying these things. What will I do so that your hands don't get cracked and sore? What will I do so that you don't die? Stand there. Useless. Completely incapable of helping you.

PRELUDE

Read at Kristiansand Library that real life can't hold a candle to life in literature. I am in real life. I get to bath Mum just before her 85th birthday on 12th February 2006. Hold her thin bird-like body. Wash it with a damp sponge. There is oil and bath salt in the warm water. Her skin is paper-thin. I have to be careful. Especially on her legs, where she has sores. Folds of skin with memories of muscle. Small, scrawny breasts. The hairs turn towards their roots. My child-crone. I wash your hair. I spread cream on your back. Your feet. Legs. Thighs. Your stomach and arms. Everything will be gone.

I travel backwards and forwards to Kristiansand. To poor mother creature, my beloved Mum. The grand-children and we four siblings travel backwards and forwards. A kind of travelling personal care team. Especially we three sisters travel. This is no time for the battle of the sexes. Personal care is at stake.

We are not so good at co-ordinating the journeys. – A mother can take care of ten children, but ten children can't take care of one mother, or something like that, says Mum with cunning triumph. We usually stay for a few days at a time, and are allowed to clean and cook. Mum also gives us permission to accompany her on walks, shopping and going on errands.

Her standards are very demanding. Especially when it comes to paperwork. The income tax return becomes an insurmountable and tortuous marathon. She's not on the internet. She can't use text messaging. Rheumatism in her hands makes it more and more difficult to move them with precision. From time to time I suggest that I take over some of her paperwork. She most definitely will not allow that. She will not be placed under guardianship. She wants to keep her independence. It is crucial for her.

Administration and organisation have been important in her life. Overseeing the kitchen towels. Cleaning materials. Implements. Changing beds. Cleaning windows. Organising furniture removals. Maintenance. Buying a side of pork. Garage appointments. Filling out income tax forms. Planning holidays. Parents' meetings.

David Rieff writes about his late mother, Susan Sontag: *Throughout her life, my mother oscillated between pride and regret over her sense of having sacrificed so much in the way of love and pleasure for her work.*

The same can be said about Mum. The difference is that Mum didn't sacrifice love and pleasure for literary or academic work, as Sontag did. Mum's work, which she undertook with a mixture of pride and bitterness, was looking after her husband and children and the places that housed them.

Now the overseeing has gone to pieces. She is continually overcome by an ostensible chaos in the cupboards and the storeroom in the cellar. She's no longer sure what she has where. What seems to us to be tidy appears to her like a rising tide of things that she no longer has control over. Everything she doesn't get done. She can't manage alone any longer. She thinks she is a burden to us, but at the same time there are rigid boundaries to what we are allowed to help with. She doesn't stop complaining. She insists on her solitude. On that, it is only we children who mean anything, but that we have *our own lives now*. We are all *so busy*. We must *certainly not come if we don't have time*. No time? Of course we have no time. We have so bloody little time, all of us, and we are so damn fed up after decades of your miserable, self-pitying whining. That nothing is ever good enough. Everything is so awful. So eternally difficult and complicated. No matter how hard we go out of our way to be pleasant. Kind. Helpful. Loving. Caring. It is never good enough. And so we become difficult. Terribly sulky and obstinate, inadequate, underachieving children.

Am so gasping for clear as glass air to breathe into my tender, all too tight lungs. Brush you away. Poor mother-creature.

Again I am sitting on the train between Oslo and Kristiansand. I know the stretch off by heart. I feel sick with the tilting on the many bends. Try to work on my laptop. Drangedal Station. Monotonous recognition. Sunshine and new-fallen snow. Houses. Cars. Road working machines that seem thrown aside. Wheezing from the seat next to mine. Someone dark-skinned. Perhaps Tamil. He speaks fluent American, I heard earlier. Sleeping soundly with a red T-shirt on. Would like to stroke his smooth, thick hair. At twelve o'clock I'll be in Kristiansand. Mum said on the telephone: – You'll soon come to regret that I don't die more quickly. Why do you come in the middle of the week and take time off work?

Who does she think she is? Placenta. *Mutterkuchen*. Motherfucker.

*A*s far as one can understand, there has been a great deal of conflict between the marriage partners for many years. The patient has had contact with Dr. (. . .), who has, according to the patient, advised her to separate. However, she cannot face doing this.

(28.01.1987, patient case file, general practitioner.)

Why don't you leave, Mum? – I asked from about six years old as I sat on the opposite side of the kitchen table with its waxed tablecloth, when she complained about her intolerable marriage. At other times she told of how they had met each other just after the war. On a bridge in Kongsvinger. One summer day. Swish, swish, Mum cycled past Dad on the bridge. His warm, brown eyes met hers. It was a love story.

Years of conflict. Sufferings that she confided in me, her handpicked witness. She and I. A river of words. A sickly cocktail of affection and unwieldy secrets. Did she have no one else to talk to? No one to confide in? Go out! Take your handbag with money, lipstick, car keys and cigarettes and go! Anywhere at all. To meet some-one. Go to the cinema or to eat cake. Shopping and chattering. Meet a lover or borrow one. Go on a trip.

16

Read the newspaper in the park. Go on a demonstration march. Go into a bar. To the hairdresser's. Go to the dogs. So that I can come back to myself. Oh Mum, don't tell me, tell me, why you are so sad? Don't tell me, tell me, why you are crying? Don't tell me, tell me, why you are sighing so quietly? Don't tell me, tell me, about your black eye? Don't tell me, tell me everything.

Sometimes, certainly, there was talk of fighting. So ugly. Not to be discussed. We preferred not to talk about it. Or about his other women.

Yes, I also really loved Dad. Every night. Long into my childhood, I came padding over and slipped into Dad's warmth. Two spoons. On the level. Preferable by far to the intense motherwarmth. Beneath her duvet. Overbearing. Not like that with Dad's warmth. Perfect temperature. A demand-free zone.

Mum did not leave. Long-drawn-out sympathy. Cold contempt. From me. She submitted. She licked his boots. She feared him. She despised him. She vilified him. She made us afraid of him. It was acutely infectious. A sneaking, venereal disease. The air distended with the anxiety of wife and children.

– **P**oor Mum, I am saying. I had heard her crying through the crack at the door to the children's bedroom. Lay in bed and listened to the restrained whimpering from the kitchen. Run barefoot in my nightdress across the parquet floor of the corridor and into the kitchen. – You poor thing, I say with tentative sympathy in my voice. The cold from the floor tiles in the kitchen rises through my legs. Go to put my arms around her, as she stands bent over the kitchen sink. Where dirty cups are never left lying. – Go to bed! Such a harsh voice. Does she not recognise me? Brushes me away. I who shall draw my sword for you, Mum. Am I in your way?

D ad didn't need any armour bearer. He was king and monster in an alluring and terrifying amalgam. I knew what it was like to be triumphant up on the warm, broad shoulders of Dad's leather jacket. To be rocked to the rhythm of his movements and steady breathing. View over everything. Sitting in the backseat. Stretched out arms. Played with the dark hair. It curled at the nape if it had been a while since he had been to the barber's. Ran and jumped on him when he lay resting on the settee after work. Flew into his arms. To tickle and be tickled. To carry on and be fooled about with. To fight and be held tight. Sparkling play of light and recognition in his eyes. Not so with Mum. Her body: not for play. Everything was working time. *Kein Feierabend*. Loving. Practical. Always taken up with compelling, necessary tasks. Extremely responsible. Considerate. Absolutely dependable. Guarantee. Mother's guarantee. Cast iron contract. Wage agreement. No fuss.

Dad: born 1916 in Maribor, Slovenia. Youngest son of an Austrian lawyer, Lothar Mühleisen. His mother: daughter of a Slovenian farming family, Elisabeth Kumer. The relationship was kept secret for many years. A son of the Austrian bourgeoisie didn't mix with Slovenian peasants. Dad had three older sisters, all born outside marriage. Immediately after the chaos that came with the First World War, grandfather acknowledged his family and got married. Dad was born within wedlock. He studied in Austria to be a civil engineer during the Second World War. His three sisters got no education. They would get married in any case.

Mum: born in 1921 in Vennesla, southern Norway. Youngest daughter of a doctor, Thorvald Fugelli. After his first wife's death, he married Gudrun Rolsdorph from Kongsvinger. Mum had three older brothers. All got financial support for academic education. But not Mum. She would get married anyway. Instead she did a one-year domestic science course and one year of commercial studies.

Mum and Dad got married in Stavanger, in the St Petri Church, in 1950. They had four children over a period of fourteen years.

The middle classes were self-contained, whether it was in Norway, Austria, Switzerland or Germany. The countries we moved about in. It was quiet. Especially quiet in Germany. No TV at our house. The radio was not switched on. Never any magazines or comics at home. A newspaper now and again. Everything was correct. Careful. Polite. Private. You didn't talk about the war. At least not in my family. At least not in the families we knew. Only later, when I realised that the fifties, in which I had grown up, were right after the war, did I realise that it was as if people in Germany were holding their breath: if we behave decently. If we stay inside our own doors, and say hello nicely to each other. If we mind our own business. If we don't get mixed up in the affairs of others. Cultivate the garden. Wash the car and hands before meals. If we dress well and earn money. Then perhaps everything will be all right. People went around like hospitalised wild animals. Apathetic wanking orang-utans, just like the ones I saw once in Amsterdam Zoo at the beginning of the 1980s. Stink of stress. With no indication of aggression, enjoyment or release. No-orgasm country. Ach, Jelinek. Where were you?

In Norway the atmosphere was a bit cheerier. Coming to Norway on summer holiday, to the summer cottage at Jæren, was like coming into a frivolous light. *Krone*-ice-cream and *Polly* peanuts. The grown-ups smiled for no reason. Were not so formal. Not so strict. The bodies took up more space. The clothes hung a bit more loosely. Children were spoken to. Much later, I understood that in Norway, of course people talked about the war. A lot to talk about. A great deal to build up. Do. A sense of community. A future to be shaped. On the right side. But not even in Norway did we talk in my family about the war. Only in 1978, when I was 25 years old and lived in an artists' commune in Austria, did I get to know. Dad paid me a visit. We went to a café together. He said he had something he must tell me. I thought I had a half-brother or sister I didn't know about. Tantalising thought. He showed me a small black-and-white photograph of a young man in uniform. He told me that he had been a soldier on the side of the Germans. So what?

I believe that my parents had a silent agreement not to speak to us about Dad's service in the German army, and therefore we didn't talk about the war in the way that everyone else in Norway did at that time. My parents met right after the war. So Mum was actually dangerously close to the category of 'German slut'. – Was it not risky for you to begin a relationship with a man who had been in the German army? Did he really make out that he was a Yugoslavian in a hard-labour camp? You realised eventually that he had been on the German side? – Well, yes . . . – What did you think? – No. . . . I didn't think like that. The war was over. Most of all, I felt sorry for him. He and his family lost everything after Slovenia was broken up. They fled to Austria.

*It is not to do with guilt, but only with the
realisation of something. Quite simply. Only
for the sake of sanity, for the sake of decency,
so to speak.*

(IMRE KERTÉSZ)

M um told me eventually that what bothered her
particularly about Dad's service on the German
side was that he never spoke to her about it. So she
provoked him at times. Even though it was dangerous.

I was about five years old. We were visiting Dad's
Slovenian mother Elisabeth, known as Oma. In Grundlsee, Austria, where the family had fled from Slovenia after
the end of the war. The little castle, Villa Castiglioni, is
situated on the shady side of the idyllic lake Grundlsee,
after which the place is called. From 1943 to 1945, it
served as the "Library of the Führer", with more than
55,000 books. These were protected from the bombing
raids on Germany in the final years of the war. The castle is
surrounded by high alpine mountains. As a child, I always
thought that the castle floated in a sinister, dark and damp
atmosphere. With its small, pointed spires, it looked as
though it had been cut right out of a vampire film.

My sister and I lay in Oma's bed beneath the crucifix with the almost naked Jesus, through the wall from the living room. The wooden shutters were closed in front of the windows, which lay open to the dark summer night. The sound of the grasshoppers enveloped the murmuring of voices that came from the grown-ups' conversation in the room beside us. Knew that there sat uncles, aunts, Mum, Dad and Oma round the big dining table. The tiled ceramic stove in the corner. Drinking wine. Green two-litre bottles of white wine on the dining table that was always covered with a white tablecloth. Snacks of Hungarian garlic sausage. Talking and laughing together. The murmur of voices all of a sudden became rough and loud. The volume increased. Sudden silence. The bedroom door opened. Mum came running in and threw herself on the bed between us. She was crying. Her hands on her face. The next day, she had a black eye. Many years later I learned that she had challenged Dad that evening to talk about his participation in the war. At Oma's dining table. In his intimate circle. In Grundlsee. Peaceful idyll of nature. Popular retreat of painters and tourists. On the opposite side of the water from the Führer's Library.

It would never have occurred to me to feel sorry for Dad. In no way did he appeal to sympathy. He did not invite any speculation about his person. He was a closed, independent individual. Never spoke of feelings. Or what he called "sentimentality". There was no question about how he was. He was. Moreover he possessed a strength that could be construed as determination. This determination demanded respect because it held the possibility of the exercise of power within it. But the energy was not only restricting. It contained an expansive, vigorous potential. And that made him both attractive and dangerous. His energy was obviously directed out to the world. He watched the news. He read newspapers. And he sat for hours in his chair and read books. Especially crime novels. Specific titles that seemed alluring: *Die Dame in Chinchilla, Der letzte Besucher, Das andere Gesicht, Das Schicksal in Person, Lauter reizende alte Damen, Die Morde des Herrn ABC*. Or he, literally speaking – whenever he liked – took his hat and went. That is to say, he sat in his car. He drove away without saying where or why. He was a free man.

It is not correct. That he was free. He behaved as though he was a free man – and that is of course a kind of freedom. Perhaps at the end of the day that is exactly the point. How you take up space. He sat in his arm-chair in the sitting room. None of the other chairs had an owner. He sat with his back to the light from the window and read. His left arm rested on the arm of the chair. Relaxed. His right held the crime novel. Legs comfortably spread out. A peaceful sight that filled the sitting room with a predetermined order. In the back-ground there was the sound of Mum's pottering and clattering in the kitchen. I didn't want her to disturb him. I was aware of being on guard. Dad was resting easily in his body with the weight and inevitability of a large animal. I had experienced that the aggression could be unleashed at the speed of lightning. From my simple presence in the room. It is possible that it was just this knowledge that caused the feeling of happiness when his playful attention was directed to-wards me, in passing as it were, as pure excess.

But he really did adapt himself. Fulfilled his duty. Provided for his family, although Mum also contributed eventually. Dad had a position as a divisional manager. This certainly involved responsibility and perhaps in addition a certain scope for freedom of action. But, most of all, predetermined tasks. Pressure from superiors. From the conversations I overheard, I understood that he was always in conflict with his bosses. Worst of all: he was bored. Long-drawn-out boredom. He put up with it. The discoveries, excesses, traumas, lay behind him. In his youth. In the war that he did not talk about. The rest was adjustment. Necessity. A kind of self-imposed propriety.

Mum recounted that, in the beginning of their mar-riage, after I was born, my sister was two years old and we lived in Dale in Hordaland; she came home one late winter afternoon to an empty flat. A premonition led her to open Dad's wardrobe – which was almost empty. She found a note. It said: "Travelling to Australia. You and the children can perhaps follow later." Mum got her mother, Gudrun, to look after us and went to Dad's family in Austria. There she got hold of him in the end. He had bought a one-way ticket to Australia. What was he going to do there? He had restlessness in his blood. Wanted to start over. Away from Europe, the past and the family. Be his own boss again. Mum persuaded Dad to accompany her home to Norway. Dale textile factories. Life as a family provider.

The last time that Dad tried to free himself, burn his bridges, strike out into the unknown, was a few years before he retired. He had driven the trade union to distraction at the Høie textile factories in Kristiansand. He was in charge of the printing department. The conflict came to a head, I think, when he had asked an employee who had an unnaturally high consumption of rubber gloves, if he was in the habit of eating them. Dad disappeared without a trace. He phoned Mum after a few days. From somewhere on the way south to Europe. She begged him to come back to the family. To her. To Kristiansand. To Høie textile factories. He did that. Buttered his lunch-pack. Went to work. Accepted that his punishment for the dispute with the trade union was a reduction in his salary and standing.

Dad died in 1996. After three heart attacks and pancreatic cancer. At Kristiansand Hospital. While I sat on a chair. Beside his bed. A well-brought-up angel of death beside a polite corpse.

I speak two languages.
Mother's language. Father's language.
Norwegian. German.

Written German is a perfectly composed language deal-ing with completely ordinary things. *Einerseits war es ihm recht, dass Ruth nicht beischlafen wollte, anderseits ärgerte er sich über die Unmöglichkeit, darüber vorher eine sachliche Übereinkunft zu erzielen, und sich zwei-tens auch noch abweisen zu lassen für etwas, was er selbst nicht wollte.*

I don't dare to write in German. Don't speak of it. Only speak it. That is absolutely certain. Father's lan-guage. The language of the law. It is not possible to cheat. Then I will be seen through. That would be certain.

It is not like that with Norwegian. Mother's language. I only need to get started. It is not the discourse of truth. I only need to begin writing. It is of course childish talk. For example, I can walk along Orrestranda shore one January morning at half past nine, where the sun hangs obliquely and all the small stones that have been washed up by the winter surf have their own ridge of sand

30

formed by the wind. And in the morning sun, each one of them has its own pyramid-shaped shadow. I walk there then, with the January wind freezing my forehead, without realising that I am talking singsong in Norwegian, while I am looking out to sea where the Orreelva river flows out.

In the beginning it was Norwegian that was spoken to me. By Mum. By grandmother Gudrun. For the short time she was there. By big sister with her two years of Norwegian. Perhaps my Dad spoke a little German to me. It has probably not been so much. He was of course, despite everything, at the factory. Dale textile factories. I was not there. I was at our lodgings with my Mum and sister. I was lying in the pram looking directly up at Mum's bright face. Directly up at the dark mountainsides. Then came the German years. When German was spoken to me at primary school. There, I wrote in German on the little blackboard that I had in my leather satchel.

In Primary 3 I learned that all this about *Muttersprache* was important. Fräulein Bill spoke about mother tongue, and I put my hand up and said proudly that my mother tongue was Norwegian. Fräulein Bill corrected this straight away. She said that Norwegian could not be my mother tongue since my father was German, we were living in Germany, and I spoke German. I insisted vehemently that my mother was Norwegian. That Norwegian was my *Muttersprache* and that my father was not German but Austrian, and perhaps part Yugoslavian. I was sent out into the corridor.

31

At home we spoke Norwegian with Mum and German with Dad, and German when we were sitting round the table together eating. Norwegian was a mummy's language. An at home language. A secret language. Baby talk. A prattling language. I was never corrected.

Talk to me, Mum, with your mummy voice. Whisper and sing to me. Kiss forth that one word. The other word. The language of love, suffering and devotion.

Talk to me, Dad, with your chesty voice. I drink up every single word. Set me free from her at the speech drought time. Talk me into reason.

I lie back in the bathtub and let the warm water rise. Millimetre by millimetre the water snuggles up my skin so that it envelops me and makes my contours yield and dissolve as my warmth meets that of the water. The bathtub expands generously. I am floating. Unfolding cell by cell. Sinking backwards. Rocking as though in amniotic fluid.

The sound of my radio reaches through the bathroom wall. I know that Mum is sitting at the kitchen table on the red adjustable chair she has been given by the disability service. With her blue-grey metal wheeled walking frame beside her. Ready. No places without the walking frame any more. Simple body technologies. From a tricycle to a walking frame. Fast forward. The red plastic gripper tool is attached to a kind of arm that helps her to pick up things on the kitchen table and worktop. The tobacco – *Eventyrblanding* and *Rizzla* cigarette papers – is lying in the drawer of the bench behind her; a half-cup of lukewarm filter coffee – *Friele* – and a lit tea-light in a little glass holder are sitting on the table. Some papers are lying there too: post, bank statements, receipts and all the memos. She writes long strings of words on yellow post-it notes and little sheets

33

of paper about what she has to do, and scores out what has been accomplished. Her handwriting is barely legible because of the rheumatism in her hands. I have put out a glass of water and a plate with grapes, a piece of banana and a peeled apple for her.

She listens to the news and the weather forecast many times a day on the silvery-grey, grating little transistor radio from the 1970's. She has some kind of fixation on the weather. It comes from the fact that, until quite recently, she still drove a car, but she didn't dare to go out in bad visibility or slippery conditions. The car was her freedom. She could drive the 18 kilometres to Flekkerøya to "Villa Soffi". Soffi was her childhood nickname – for Ellen Sofie. She bought this summer-house outside Kristiansand for us four children in 1990. She furnished it as a kind of museum of our family history. Family photographs on the walls. Of children, grandchildren, and of many of the houses and flats we have lived in. The summerhouse was a type of re-creation. An evocation. An admonition. A common denominator. Essence. Substratum. Archive. The place was meant to have a magnetic effect and draw her children to her. Where they had once felt at home. Feel at home? *Unheimlich*.

She put a lot of energy and thought into keeping the house in good repair. Tidying, cleaning, fixing, hanging up lists of how the mains stop-cock should be turned on, the anti-freeze filled up, the cellar door locked, and how the house should be left for the next user. She had also cut out little poems and sketches from newspapers. In these she usually wrote that we should be friends and

34

sleep well. The house was never completely ours. She was the manager and curator of the museum.

She is calling me. I shout back that I'll be finished soon. Direct the single jet of water from the shower, which is slightly warmer than the water around me, on to my clitoris. Take a deep breath, lean my head backwards into the water and meet the jet of water in the same movement. Stand up in the bathtub. The mirror is covered in steam. – I'll come right away now, I call, while I grab a bath towel.

Early morning at Oslo Central Station. I am coming straight from Kristiansand. Since I am at the bottom of the escalator in the airport train departure hall, I direct my gaze upwards and see a young boy who is throwing something away with an abrupt movement; he closes his eyes and moves slowly backwards in an arc. The banister in the middle of his back. He sways like this in a fragile balance with his face up and his head back above the escalator where I am standing. I run to reassure myself that he won't fall down or maybe has stopped breathing. As I grab his jacket to hold him tightly, I see that his ribcage is rising and falling slowly and evenly in the midst of this unnatural position. His features are soft, child-like, and have a completely peaceful, yes – blissful expression. Carefully, I displace his centre of gravity towards the banister so that he, with my support, slides down towards the floor. Glance furtively around me hoping that no security guard will put my angel out of paradise and into the early winter morning at Oslo Central Station.

G rey, damp winter light behind the windowpane. A dream of coming home still remains. Someone has moved furniture and objects and this has made my home disturbingly unfamiliar. Awaken because of a spot on my shoulder that is radiating a slight, concentrated pain. Lift up the duvet and feel the air of the cold winter night on my skin. It hits a thin damp filter layer of perspiration. The pattern on the wood panelled wall always meets my eyes when the alarm clock rings. Sit up in the bed. Look at the snow outside. If it rains, there will be too much weight on the roofs. Hard work to clear away the waterlogged snow.

As I move my upper body, I feel stiffness combined with slight tenderness in my limbs. Remember what it's like to be inside my childhood self. Body without a past. No baggage or memories deposited in sinews, muscles, cells. Hardly a scar. Perfectly at one with my intentions. Completely without ulterior motives. Second thoughts. Running barefoot across the sun-warmed, grass-covered drive that stretched 200 metres along the fence. My child feet hardly disturbed the hard-trampled grass, and the warm air pressed softly on my skin when I increased my speed. The scent of sun-warmed grass floated like a gentle liquid around me. Fingers of wind through my hair. Was well aware that I could run as fast as I wanted to. As long as I wanted. Wherever I wanted to go. My breath squeezed through my lungs, smarting a little when I picked up speed. Just like when the yellow lemonade powder I used to buy in the shop tingled bitter-sweetly on my tongue. I wanted more air in my lungs and accelerated to feel the lemonade powder air force itself in.

Now I take with me a towel that has been left behind as I move my body, stiff with sleep, down the stairs. Into the bathroom. Six degrees outside. I'll have half an hour at work to prepare a meeting. If I'm to get hold of a cheap ticket to Kristiansand, I must make the booking today. Standing in front of the mirror. Before me lies a trail of morning routines. I can change the order of them, but automatic action brings efficiency. Someone has used up my shampoo. The warm water on my face. Then ice-cold water. Stroke the back of my head. Put a tampon in my pocket. How many times have I menstruated? The sinking, dull, slightly painful enjoyment of the contractions in my womb; the tiredness, the sluggishness, the desire to collapse into myself. The headache. The body's regained lightness afterwards. Feelings of lighthearted freedom, in the certainty of the interval until the next time. The future without a cycle, possibly a constant feeling of lightheartedness.

After two nights of dreaming that I am carrying her and feeding her, she telephones to ask me to leave her alone. She has to sort something. So many papers. She has to read something, and she can't have someone at her house all the time – I am still living, she says.

38

So alive you were, Mum! Slim, tall, refined. Always well turned out. Eccentric in your combination of clothes. 1959. Aalen. West Germany. I am six years old. You have bought your own car! A tiny, little four-seater with the brand name *Prince*. Light grey. No one has such a cool little car in the street where we live. None of the mummies has a car at all. It is summer. You are wearing the yellowish-green trousers. They stop a little below the knees. With a small split in the sides. A tiny black edge sewn around the split. Fine black stripes in the poplin-type material. White sleeveless top. Green silk scarf around your neck. Flat shoes. Mid-length, blonde hair with a light perm. A trace of make-up. Red lipstick. You are standing beside "The Prince", as the car is called from now on. You have tooted your horn so that my sister, with our youngest sister in her arms, and I come running out. You laughingly pose in front of the car. With an elegant cigarette in your hand. We shout with joy. You invite us on a maiden trip round the neighbourhood.

I accuse you, Mum: you lingered in an absurd, deeply dependency-creating love for your children. This love drained your vitality. Reduced you to a self-pitying existence. Are we both without responsibility? You for your helpless suffering? I for my fury and my conscience-stricken contempt?

Homemade mashed potatoes with fried egg and tomato sauce. A woollen blanket under the quilt in winter and clean bedclothes after bath time on Fridays. Clean clothes in the cupboards. You bought clothes for us. You sewed clothes. You knitted. You always got up before everyone and made the breakfast. I heard your footsteps in the flat and rattling from the kitchen after I had gone to bed. You bought all the food. You made all the meals for us every day. You buttered lunch-packs for school. You made up the picnics for the beach: orange juice, raw carrot and wholemeal bread with *Sunda* honey spread. Sweet little windfall tomatoes from the greenhouses. Sand from Orrestrand beach mixed in with the sandwiches and crunched between our teeth. Whisked egg with lots of sugar made from eggs from the farm across the river. Always you wanted to know how I was. That I was fine. You talked to me. You phoned me. You wrote letters to me.

I would so much like to look after you a bit, now that you are old and sick and are going to die. You are all alone, after all. Put a woollen blanket in your bed and make you a fried egg. Phone you and ask how you are. Write you a letter.

DEATH

When you die, Mum. I am preparing myself. When you die, Mum. I have tried to prepare myself for a few years. I have not managed to reshape the living you into a representation of a dead body. A corpse. An impossibility. Everything you know about me. You know about events I can't reach back to. They won't let themselves play back. You have a conversion program deep inside you of which there is only one copy. When you die, Mum, what I don't know will be erased.

Under the pillow you placed a letter from each of your children and grandchildren. The letters lay there when you died.

In the final weeks, Mum became so frail that she spent most of the time lying on the settee waiting to die. She said she hadn't thought that it would go so fast. Sometimes a grandchild or a son-in-law came in and sat down on one of the chairs around the side table. Then she opened her eyes, looked for a long time at this person who had arrived, spoke the name a few times in a weak voice, closed her eyes again and said: – No, now you are whining, Ellen.

S it immovable by the low coffee table and watch Mum, who is lying on the settee. The time she spends at the kitchen table is reduced, and the extent of her movement around the flat has shrunk. The space around a dying person decreases in proportion to the movement towards complete standstill. There is, without doubt, a final place. I imagine a map marked with the places she has been, and with lines between the points. One place on this map is a last point. We are very close to the last marking on the map of Mum's life. – I am so tired, she says. In the end, she hardly manages to speak. Moving her tongue exhausts her. More a faint muttering.

She is wearing the thin, mustard-yellow polo-necked jumper and beige cotton leggings. These are the last clothes she wears. Apart from the nightdress I put on her the day before she dies, after I had cut up the yellow polo-neck and the fine silk vest underneath, because I couldn't manage to pull the jumper over her head. That she resisted. Either the choice of nightdress or wearing anything at all, but I don't think I could have let her lie there completely naked.

But now Mum is still lying on the settee with two

cushions under her head, one cushion under her feet, because her heels are so painful. She is covered by two blankets, one green and one red. There is a glass of water on the coffee table. The cordless telephone that gives access to her children and grandchildren, and the red alarm clock that keeps time for her, are placed strategically around her. She looks as if she is sleeping, but she is not. She throws both the blankets off. That means that she wants to sit up. I help her to swing her legs down, while I hold her around her back. Must be so careful. She has sores on her legs because her skin is so thin. Everything will go to pieces. She sits up with difficulty, reaches out her hand in slow motion towards the glass of water, which I quickly pick up for her. Drinks a few small sips, and the next thing is that she wants to go to the toilet.

This is three days before she dies. She can still move with the help of a wheeled walking frame if she has assistance. It goes very slowly and is unspeakably laborious for her. She will not hear of a wheelchair, even though there is a real danger that she will fall. In the course of the next day, she gets a wheelchair that I have smuggled into the flat without her knowledge. When I first say, quite decidedly, that I can't manage any longer to go back and lift her while she clings to the walking frame and collapses more and more, she agrees, two days before she dies, to sit in the wheelchair.

But this is the day before the wheelchair. It is also the day before the commode which I have sitting in readiness, so that I can avoid having to carry her all the way to the toilet. This she resists even more vociferously. She

48

only got to use that chair for half a day. She lay in bed for the last two days, and neither on my own nor with help – the few times it came – did I manage to get her up, despite her repeated and insistent calls.

One day before all this she is sitting on the settee. Has drunk her small sips of water. Now she gives a sign that she wants to move. I take her under her arms, count to three while I lift her, and she holds on to the handles of the walking frame. I go directly behind her, with legs akimbo, and hold her and lift her at the same time, while she walks the now-so-long distance to the bathroom. Once she watched over my first steps. Now I watch over her last. The last steps carry no promises in them.

When we reach the toilet, she is completely exhausted and shaking. She calls out to me, and I have to stand beside her. She is scared. Is she afraid all the time? I no longer ask her about anything other than the totally mundane. – Are you thirsty? Are you hungry? Are you in pain? The words draw the strength from her body.

On the way back to the settee, we walk past the kitchen, and I try to get her to sit in her chair at the kitchen table. Perhaps I can persuade her to eat a few teaspoons of yogurt. Yogurt is the only thing she eats now. Just like when she was pregnant with my brother. We lived in Switzerland. I was twelve years old. She asked me over and over again to run to the shop and buy yogurt for her. Natural yogurt. Fourth child. Forty-five years old. Mum was proud that she had such a little bump when she was expecting. – Like a little football, she said with satisfaction. When I was pregnant and became enormous, she shook her head triumphantly over my sorry state.

49

I manage to persuade her to sit down. Doesn't want to eat. I ask her if she would like a puff of a cigarette. She shakes her head. I swallow tears. She has *always* smoked, even though she desperately tried in recent years to give up, and thought of it as a terrible defeat of self-will that she failed to do so. For the last little while she rolled her cigarettes with trembling hands. Took a few puffs. Clipped off the glowing end with a pair of scissors over a glass of water. Afraid of fire. I stand and wait. She indicates dully that she would like to go back to the settee. I see that she gathers strength she doesn't have, to manage to go the distance. We manage it. She sits on the settee. I swing her round by holding her around her back and lifting her legs up at the same time. First the red blanket, then the green. Place the cushion under her feet. She falls asleep from exhaustion. I sit at the table and watch over her until she wants up the next time. It happens soon. This was our choreography. Last waltz.

Our first point of contact without a shared circulation of blood took place at our lodgings in Dale. Came to pass suddenly with a premature birth. I had the umbilical cord round my neck, and was being strangled. – *Ich kann dieses Kind nicht sehen*, was Dad's observation when he saw my blue face and closed the door. I looked deformed after the near-strangulation.

85 years ago, Mum was born in Vennesla. She does not know how it feels to be born. She knows how it feels to give birth. That is something we have in common.

Not peaceful. But with heartrendingly earnest resistance, without any prospect of success, she loses her grip on herself. You're not having it, Mum! I certainly don't have a hold on myself, either! I always come to myself too late, whereas you have insight into the roots of my existence. You were the habitat. The organiser. The mover. The brutality. Symbiosis and separation in one. The first frontier. Although you did not rule over your own self, you knew more about my not-yet self than I at any time get to know. Therefore you are in possession of an indulgent love for me that I cannot expect from anyone else.

Now I am lying beside you once more. After 53 years,

our bodies, somewhat changed, are lying together again in the one bed. 53 years ago, we were both in dramatic transitional circumstances. You in the fundamental, incomprehensible state of reproducing oneself. Redoubling. Multiplying. Repeating. Force out an organic creature grown from your own tissue. Now, once again, both in a dramatic crossing over. Here it is life that will be wound up. Now it is I who am *in charge*, but that's not how I experience it. Perhaps you did not either, that time at our lodgings in Dale. You have recounted that you were looking forward to a stay at a maternity hospital. A kind of well-deserved housewife's holiday. With regular meals and other people to look after the housekeeping.

The longed-for recuperation came to nothing since I arrived early. I was born at home. There is uncertainty here about the facts. The local midwife managed to accelerate the birth at our lodgings, as she was anxious to fit in another birth on the same day. Got paid by piecework. She gave Mum something that was illegal – I think it was strychnine? – to make the birth go faster. Her scheming action would nevertheless turn out to be in the interests of Mum and me, for neither the midwife nor Mum could know about the umbilical cord being round my neck prior to my appearance, as ultrasound technology, the scanning method – one aspect among many that means that today we would not be entrusted in this way to midwives with their listening horns and strychnine in their cases – had not yet been invented.

When I am lying now beside you once more, there is no midwife with strychnine here. Instead I have a small, blue case lying underneath your bed, which I have been handed the day before by the "Pain Relief Team" as the group is called in Kristiansand. The team consists of an oncologist and a nurse, with whom I have had only one conversation. I miss the presence of a midwife. There is morphine in this case, together with anti-spasmodic and sedative medicines. I learned yesterday how to administer the morphine through a needle that is attached near her spine. Not strychnine, but morphine. This time too in order to ease (hasten?) her passage. You, who gave birth to me, are now dying with me. If you gave me life, I am giving death. I am not a midwife. A deathwife. I ease your pains. You do not want morphine because you are afraid of becoming dependent, but you don't have time for that to happen. You are so weak that you cannot protest, or perhaps you don't notice when I sneak up behind your back and let the morphine spread through your tissues.

The case is under the bed. At times of birth and death there is not the distinction between night and day that there is otherwise. We pretend that it is night time. And so I am lying on the bed. In the double bed by Mum's side. Trying to sleep. Each time I am about to drop off, each time my all-too-present awareness mercifully breaks loose, Mum calls out: – I must! This means that she wants to get up or go to the toilet. But it has become impossible to carry this out.

I am lying beside you. Beside your body which is changing before my eyes. The process of death. The way of death. I don't really know how much pain you are in. It costs you so much to answer me. It looks as though

53

you are struggling with the primary processes. Perhaps something like myself, when I was born, only the other way around. Not facing life, but facing death.

No, it cannot be correct. That is exactly what I feel is so incomprehensible. That she, that the human being, right up to the final tenth of a second, even if it is no longer conscious – in fact whether it wants to or not – fights to live. Her heart is beating so hard in her thin, hollow body. It thunders right through everything, and her entire body, held together by the frame of her skeleton, lacks muscles and yields to the tormenting force of gravity that she once upon a time jousted against so triumphantly. Everything is shaking because of this heart, so that I have the feeling of holding her heart in my hands. Even though it is light, it is nevertheless impossible to bear.

I lie in an unguarded moment feeling so helpless. My heart is beating wildly together with yours. I have to help you. *Hilf dir selbst so hilft dir Gott.* I think that you are in fact sleeping. Weeping without a sound. As I turn my head, I see that you are gazing at me with a cold, noticing look. You have seen everything. You have seen my helplessness now when I should be strong for you. Now you understand where things are going. I feel ashamed to witness that you are losing everything.

There you took the last trick. I am standing here with your excrement on my hands. Your brave little helper. Why are you screaming like that? *My* roaring could fill this whole room. *I* can clutch your thundering heart. I can tear it to pieces. Can leave you to lie here, alone. Turn away at the door. Then you can die.

I have to hurry. Open the window. Air. Fetch some fruit juice to have in the glass. Check if I have enough nappies. I must take the opportunity to go to the toilet. Hurry and eat something. She can waken at any time. Have an irresistible urge for a cup of coffee. Standing in the kitchen. Looking out of the window. At the familiar view of the blocks of flats on the other side of the street. A woman. Beige quilted coat, carrier bags. Opening up the entrance door. Perhaps she'll watch TV tonight. She doesn't know what is happening here in this flat. People die all the time.

Should you pull yourself together when you are dying? A considerate death? Or is it then that you can truly give in? Really not give a damn. Buddhist monks gather their nearest and dearest around them when they decide that it is time to die. They design this planned event with care. I heard that on the radio.

There is no aesthetic of death at Mum's deathbed. Crude death struggle. And the stench of death.

My brother and I stand bent over Mum. He and my eldest daughter arrived a few hours ago. There are seven hours to go until she dies. We don't know that. We understand that it has to happen soon. We are trying to interpret her outbursts. Loud cries for help. She shouts for us even though we are standing right beside her bed. She screams: – I must! Sometimes: – Mother! My brother and I try to calm her. We say: – We are with you. We are here. I say: – We are looking after you. Then she directs her knife-like look at me. She hisses: – Looking after! She is right. *Recht hat sie. Wir hassen sie.* If the cap fits.

Directly after my brother calls me and my daughter into the bedroom to be with him when she dies, directly after she ceases to breathe, directly after we stand – uncertain for how long – staring at her without saying anything; directly afterwards we walk wordlessly – as though by arrangement – and purposefully into the kitchen. Sit round the table. Search out what we can find by way of alcohol in Mum's cupboard. Start drinking. My brother drinks sherry. My daughter red wine. I cognac. We drink quickly. Talk harshly. Talk to each other loudly. We laugh boisterously at the glaring incompetence and absence of the community nurse service. We sneer contemptuously at our great sense of anxiety. We talk at a furious pace about Mum's physical disintegration. About our amateurish taking turns with the morphine. The worry that she might become dehydrated. About her unfathomable sense of panic. Her cries. Her fleeting moments of complete lucidity. About how she saw through our helplessness. Her powerlessness. Loneliness. There is a pact around the table. We have been participants. Witnesses. We do not call ourselves the "Pain Relief Team". Our name is "The Team from Hell". After the binge, we go to bed. We sleep a short – we sleep a heavy – slumber. Mum is lying in the next room. She is dead.

The radical unwinding of the bodily functions. The implosion of matter. The deprogramming of the cells. Her useless refusal, the physical pains and the panic about the grotesquely quick countdown over a few days, all were so overwhelming that the customary constructions of meaning about death have collapsed for me. I see no connection between them and what I saw, heard, and smelled.

The intervals between each breath are often so long now that it seems absurd that the dying person might take yet another breath, do not become anxious when the dying person coughs and fights for breath when she can't get enough air, it is all exactly as it should be, the actual cause of death is almost always suffocation, do not be worried if she wets herself.

(Sara Stridsberg)

Is it mere chance how one dies?

Now I am searching for the signs of death on my own body. Whoever seeks, shall find.

NOCTURNE

I think of you in the way I hear music that was recorded a long time ago. You are completely real. I say your name, and you are there.

One sister comes from Oslo. One from London. Youngest daughter and son-in-law from Oslo. You have to come when Mother is dead. We follow the new arrivals into the bedroom. There lies Mum, curled in her last position. We see them look. We don't really know what to do with ourselves.

We are waiting for the undertakers to carry her out. We prepare food. We sit together. My brother lights a candle in the bedroom, where Mum is lying. Of course! We can do that. We decide that my eldest sister should look out clothes; just like Mum always looked out clothes for us when we were little, and placed them nicely folded on a chair. Mum will wear the clothes in the coffin. Later. There is a fumbling, matter-of-fact atmosphere. At regular intervals, I go back. Into the room with the cold stench. Open window. Stand by the bed. Look at her for the last time. Once more for the last time. One more time. In the still intact bedroom. With the photographs of her parents. Dad. Us children. Grandchildren. I run my hand over the chest of drawers. She had this with her from her childhood home. In a few weeks' we'll be sorting out the jewellery in it. We'll put small nametags on them before we tidy out – that is to say, throw out, most of the flat.

People from the undertakers carry her out of the flat. I don't want to meet them. I don't want to watch them carry Mum out. – They were nice, my sister said.

I don't want a clergyman at my funeral, Mum said. Those hypocrites.

She is lying in the chapel at the side of the church. In an open bier. Wearing the fine angora knitted jacket that my sister had looked out for her. Hands folded over her chest. The face. The grimace of death.

A Quaker friend said a few words.

My brother said a few words.

I said a few words.

Music by Jan Johansson.

Then she was burned.

Afterwards. Coffee and open sandwiches. Conversations with relatives and friends. Some I had never met before. Others I hadn't seen for thirty, forty years.

Later I go on my own to a bar in the centre of Kristiansand and drink.

All four siblings are gathered in Mum's flat in Kristiansand a few weeks after the funeral. We have arranged to divide up her things. Empty the flat. I walk and linger through the rooms of furniture. Photographs. Pictures. Ornaments. She has lived here for twenty years. The last ten on her own. A few pieces of furniture, objects, photographs and pictures have gone along with my parents' homes since I was a child. Because I have visited them regularly, there is a residue of feeling for my childhood home in this flat. The connection of objects to the people who own them. A woollen blanket. The plates in the kitchen cupboard. Vases. Towels. Stones and shells she has collected on Orrestranda beach and other places. All the photographs of us. Of our children. Postcards. The way she kept things tidy. The flat. A boundary. A deposit left by a life lived. Collected up. Arranged by. Looked after. By her. A biographical installation. From being a living connection, absurd signs of absence.

Gefundenes Fressen for an archaeologist. But this is not an archaeological excavation. This is a dead person's estate. It is a private event. My mother was not a public person. Beyond the registers and archives in

67

which all people are recorded, as well as papers and data in connection with her as a customer, and some contributions she had written in recent years for the newspaper *Fædrelandsvennen*, for example about what an excellent job the community nursing service in Kristiansand did – although she herself never put up with being helped – beyond these traces of my mother, she is, she was, private.

A private person. Other people leave behind a life's work. A whole work of life. Sometimes even a work of art. *Lebenskunst*. We have come to wipe out this private flat. We go to work quickly and systematically. We only have one day. Some are pulling down the curtains. Others are throwing out papers. Pictures. Ornaments. Rugs. Clothes. In black bin bags. The property is being emptied. Drawers, cupboards, tallboys, are emptied out. After we have drawn lots. For a dinner set. A few pieces of jewellery. Some furniture. A picture here and there. A photograph. A pot. I get to take chairs for a dining table. A photo album. Some papers belonging to Dad. Some papers belonging to Mum. A picture Mum has painted. A bible and psalm book with her maiden name written in them. A cardigan. A pair of gloves. A jacket. Everything is going out. The flat has to be sold. There is a job to be done. I will never come back here again. The people who are going to live in the flat know nothing about Mum. They will surely have the double bed in the same place where Mum fought her struggle with death. The stains will be wiped clean. The undertakers have already sprayed the stench of death away. It will certainly be redecorated. In light, pretty colours. With a tasteful interior. They may install a fireplace. Mum had wondered last Christmas whether she should have a wood-burning stove put in. – There's nothing like the heat from a wood-burner, she said. I persuaded her that it would be too complicated with wood, emptying ash, walking frame. The whole thing. She saw that.

In the future when I walk past Strandpromenaden 9 in Kristiansand. No, I will never walk past Strandpromenaden 9 in Kristiansand. It has always been an ugly building. Kristiansand is a hideous town. Soulless. Sugar sweet. They smile and smile. They talk with light southern accents. They pretend to be friendly. Kind. Especially the Kristiansand ladies. "Pain Relief Team", as you were. A little blue plastic case with morphine, cramp-relieving medicines and sedatives. That is all you can expect in Kristiansand when you are lying there breathing your last. When you stand there alone. And watch your mother die. I have looked after the morphine. In the event of there being no fucking team with a blue case nearby the next time.

If I hear another single edifying word about meaningfulness about life stages about how things are connected if anyone asks if I'm feeling better if anyone says that it'll soon be easier that she was old that it's the way of the world that we will all die that I should do something cheerful that it's good that it wasn't a young person who died of cancer that I mustn't blame myself that it's not certain it went so badly that it's good she was able to be together with some of her family that she was lucky to live so long that I should take a holiday that it is natural that it was good she was able to let go that

70

WITHOUT END

It is two and a half months since Mum died I am so tired of being in this state after Mum's death my eyelids become warm I feel a pressure on my eyeballs when I think of her I do it all the time I have no time I can't manage I don't understand it I stroke her name with my fingers kiss the name on the bill envelopes cry won't fight it want to be there together with you smell the green blanket I took with me from the flat everything was so lovely at your house everything had its place I will always miss you I love you Mum you are so annoyingly close to me now that you are dead you have always been there

Thinking about death. A method of forestalling it. Warding it off. Prevent it from taking me by surprise. Acknowledge it. Divert it. Show respect. Flatter it. Pay for its indulgence.

When the lamb opened the fourth seal, I heard the voice of the fourth living creature say, "Come!" I looked, and there before me was a pale horse! Its rider was named Death, and Hades was following close behind him.

(The Revelation of St John)

The urn is on the chest of drawers in the summer cottage at Jæren. I have placed a candle on top of the chest. When I go to have my morning swim, I peek into the room where the urn and the candle are and say: – Now I'm going for my morning swim, Mum. Back soon. The same when I'm going on a trip in the evening to Orrevannet lake, or when I come back and say: – Hello, I'm back.

My sister drove the urn from Kristiansand to Orre yesterday. It was parcelled up in a cardboard box and sealed with tape. I didn't know what to do with the box. It will be here for two days, and I don't think I could place it under the staircase in the hallway. And so I ripped the box open. The urn resembles a large, round tin packed in small strips of paper. We shall open it tomorrow and put half of the ashes into another container. It opens like a tin of paint, by easing the lid off with a knife. The ash is white, grey and black. Small particles. Rougher than I had thought.

From time to time, I walk into the room where the urn is, to place a new candle in the candlestick. Touch the urn. Look at the pictures hanging on the walls. There is a photo hanging up, of Mum together with her brothers,

Aksel and Reidar. She is perhaps six years old in the picture. Short hair. A shy, almost smiling look. There is also a larger picture hanging over the bed. The portrait, from when she was around 10-12 years old, shows some characteristic features I recognise from many of her photographs. It shows a bright, open and at the same time slightly romantic look, past the eyes of the be-holder. Clear facial features. Posing for the camera in a way that I associate with old-fashioned film sets and portraits of women. It looked as though Mum, when she had a camera focussing in her direction, automatically affected this posture. Even when she was older. In the pictures from her youth, she looks like a blonde film star. The last time I managed to fulfil her wish to sit up in the bed – twenty-four hours before she died, I had managed to get hold of her around her back. I held my arm round her, and squeezed her tightly into me, since she didn't have the strength to raise herself on her own, so that we were sitting side by side on the edge of the bed. At the same time, I tried to feed her with teaspoons of honey water. She could no longer manage to suck liquids through a straw. It was as much as she could do to hold her head up. She sat quite still, while I felt that I was starting to get cramp in the arm that lay around her back. Endlessly slowly, like in a slow-motion film, she lifted her right arm, raised her hand and placed it under the wisps of hair at the right side of the nape of her neck and closed her eyes – as though she were going to lift her head and toss back her hair. A fragment of a lifelong habitual movement. The last time in a long, but allotted series of repetitions – then her arm fell down heavily and she could no longer manage to hold her head up. For a tenth of a second, I recognised the way of lifting her head as a pose towards eyes that met hers. Whose glance was she posing for this final time? The reproduction of vanity. To create yourself. Consideration for yourself as a fundamental concept even when the certainty of a future no longer exists.

Last summer, she sat across from me on the other side of the dining table here in the summer cottage. At that time, she had been talking to herself for four hours. In the end I broke down in tears. She stopped her flow of words for a moment, directed her gaze indifferently towards me and said: – Just you cry, and went on talking. This year, her urn is on the chest of drawers in the room where she slept last year. Last night I slept on my own together with the urn in the summer cottage. Not in the same room, but upstairs. The room faces the river that divides the summer cottage from the church-yard at the old Orre Church.

Like to hear the sound of the river while I'm falling asleep.

One more night with her ashes.

The room just beyond the living room where Mum slept for two nights last summer, when everything became so difficult. Her urn is here now. In the chest of drawers she had all of her Orre things, such as: – sewing kit, string, sticking plaster, comb, toilet paper, candles, writing paper, pens, nightclothes, warm jumpers, track-suit, scissors, towels, elastic bands, and other things that would otherwise just disappear from the summer cottage with its many users.

This evening I shall go to the beach and pick two carrier bags full of the pink and white dog roses that grow there along with all the wild flowers that Mum was so fond of. I will put the flowers into a basin of water, so that they will keep until tomorrow. Tomorrow we will first of all put the urn down on the grave at Eiganes churchyard in Stavanger, where the urns belonging to Mum's parents and Dad also lie. That is to say, we will transfer half the ash into another container. My sister has already been informed by the undertakers in Kristiansand that it is not legal to divide up the ashes in this way. It has perhaps been thought from olden days that the ash is a kind of entity that represents the person. *It is necessary to apply to the Chief Executive of the region in which the ashes are to be scattered for permission to do so. It is a condition of the scattering that it should take place in a decorous and solemn way, and that the ash is not divided, but scattered in one place only. The co-operation of the church cannot be demanded for this ceremony, and the name of the deceased cannot be included on the gravestone in the churchyard.*

(Chief Executive)

Nevertheless, Mum expressed the wish that some of her ashes, together with the urn, should be at Eiganes churchyard, and the remainder scattered on the sea at Orre, as she had requested of the Chief Executive. We have made an arrangement with a fisherman down at Obrestad harbour. If the weather holds, he has said that he is willing to take us out in the fishing boat to Orre so that we can scatter the ashes just beyond Orrestranda beach where the mouth of the river meets the sea. The remainder of the ashes.

It is just like Mum not to be able to make up her mind. She always complained that she couldn't make decisions. She became absolutely desperate in situations where she had to make a choice. Often she failed to choose. As a rule, this involved whatever she was dissatisfied with, becoming even worse. Anxiety about the unknown weighed most heavily regardless. The bitter safety of the status quo. Her last choice is turned into a both-and.

After we have scattered the ashes on the sea outside Orre (the sun made the ash glitter in a myriad of colours as the ash-particles reflected the sunlight and sank, and the wild flowers I had picked on the beach the evening before, lay like an undulating carpet on the surface of the water), my daughter gave me a roguish look from the bow of the smack, with the sun and the sky above her, stretched her arms out in midair and shouted – free at last! *Freudes Götter Funken.*

Last summer, Mum was walking around here with her wheeled walker. After a great deal of persuasion, she agreed to spend a few days at the summer cottage in Jæren. She had spent summers here since the days of her childhood and youth. With her parents. With Dad and us siblings and with the grandchildren. The place crammed with memories. Fragments. Connections. A house like a physical presence and a consciousness between those who are dead, those who still remain, and the new arrivals still to come. An offer. A command.

Something was frighteningly different. A keen sense of high spirits after a long period of low mood. All winter. Spring. No one knew that Mum had cancer. No one could give any assistance other than to offer sleeping tablets and anti-depressants, accompanied by the observation that she was old, after all. Telephone conversations. – How are you? – Terrible. Lonely. I am so dreadfully tired. I'm not feeling up to doing anything. I just hang about here. It's not normal. I don't know what's wrong with me. There's so much I ought to be doing. I can't keep things straight any more. I can't manage any longer. What's going to happen? You have your own lives now.

Then all at once her reunion with the summer cottage where *I have trod my childhood steps,* as she was wont to say. She stood bent over her walking frame with her lopsided hip and crooked back. The skies over Jæren huge above her. I realised immediately that the depression was over. She was filled with an intense energy. A final brutal all-out effort. She didn't have much time. She was purposeful in a meaningless way. I did not understand. No one understood. All expectations of peaceful days in the summer cottage, with me padding about around her in her most beloved place, were wrecked. Her energy and strength had something strange, something disconnected, about them. She was inconsiderate. That was the way she was. She who always thought about our welfare.

In the evenings she sat in a corner of the room. My brother's family and mine sat around the coffee table chatting in our easy – frivolous way. It wasn't only that. It was also a part of the reversal that happens between children and their parents. First of all, children are ruthlessly handed over to their parents. The upper hand. Always the potential for violence. Children know that their carers are their superiors. That they are living by their grace. As a rule, it goes fine. Always it goes wrong. Something goes consistently very wrong.

Then it turns. Sooner or later, it always turns. The children become adults. The parents become old, sick, weak. They don't follow what's going on. Ask stupid questions. Or – just a suggestion of doubtful remarks. Looking for confirmation. Stuck in the old world. Are not a part of the future. The new technologies. The new world order. The new threats. The new pleasures. Haven't read the books. Heard the music. Seen the films. The web pages. Don't chat online. Don't blog. Don't use email. Nor internet banking. They peer into the telephone catalogue with a magnifying glass. Their children become superior to their parents. They have the chance. For revenge. It always comes. Sometimes politely explanatory. Sometimes indulgent. With sympathy in their voices. Contempt. Sometimes humorous. Taking the mickey. Sometimes with a gleam in the eye. Other times icy. Condescending. Ironic. Sometimes with palpable aggression. – Just wait, and you'll see for yourself, said Mum when I accused her of something or other I thought she had done wrong as a mother. Now I have an idea of what she knew.

It's like that with us too. We sat there triumphantly, with the blind vitality of our cells remaining, on that bright summer evening in Jæren. The familiar view through the living room windows over the white, old Orre Church on the other side of the river. Peachy gold. Indirectly illuminated by the sun that just then lay right under the horizon. The conversation flowed gently and effortlessly among us, while the old woman with hectic roses in her emaciated cheeks sat in a corner beside the bookshelves filled with crime novels, forgotten romances, and books about Jæren, and came out with her incomprehensible comments. We didn't need to pay any attention to her. She no longer had any power over us. Had played herself out completely on the sidelines with her perpetual nagging and fussing about who should repair what and who had behaved badly or ought to be helped. Nix. Nada. Enough is enough. We clucked in self-satisfaction and sipped at our glasses of red wine.

She had lit a fire in the stove even though it was far too warm after one of those precious calm summer days in Jæren. The stored heat percolated out of walls and furniture. She lit all the candles she could find. Many. An action. A manifesto, the meaning of which we rejected, coldly and suspiciously. If only she could behave like other people. Stop making such a fuss of herself, as if everything was so significant. So laden with symbol. Always taking up difficult questions. About deep, existential matters. Solving problems. Making plans – especially practical ones. And did we have to know at all times how she was? Her innermost feelings?

I held myself aloof. I kept a calculated distance from her. She shouldn't be able to drag me into her manoeuvres. A touch of pity. But you certainly can't go on like this.

You forgot that you were our mother. Instead you became an installation artist with a few candles and your children as objects while you unravelled the stitches in your memory. Enough stitches to be able to look at us with a cold eye. Late freedom.

The next day she sat for four hours at the dining table and talked into the empty space. The wheeled walker placed next to her chair. A coffee cup. A half-eaten slice of bread and some pieces of peeled apple on a plate. Rolling tobacco. A lighter. An ashtray and a glass of water into which to drop the glowing cigarette ends. Yellow post-it notes. A pen. A roll of kitchen towel. I sat on the other side of the table. The sun through the windows moved the shadows across the table. She was not speaking to me. I don't know who she was conjuring up. Her self. She spoke in an uninterrupted stream. Monologues. Dialogues. Scenes. Dramatic situations. Calling to account. Placing on record. Exclamations. Had she gone mad? Had she in fact gone off her head? Or senile. But why so suddenly? Thoughtless. I was tired. Resigned. Angry. Feeling very sorry. I understood her. Such things just can't be comprehended.

Therefore I'm crying now. The summer afterwards.

Sitting where I sat last year, looking at the empty chair on the other side of the table. Lift my eye out through the window over towards Orre Church. The large, white barn and the white, heritage farm buildings of Jæren right beside the church. Looking for this segment. The white, geometrical surfaces are objective, demonstrative. No embellishment called forth by the position of the sun in the sky. Flat, grey, cloudy. Rain in the air. The wind compressing the grass into chronic obliqueness. Continual low pressure that does not yield.

Now I can afford to cry. To miss. To reproach myself. This summer I find the messages she left behind last year. "Thanks for having me. E.S.R.F.", standing for Ellen Sofie Rolstorph Fugelli. She included her initials all over the place. On one note it says: "Till we meet again." On another, "To think that I got to see my beloved old summer cottage again." In the cottage guest book, a drawing on a yellow post-it note. A heart with an arrow through it. Coloured in red with a colouring pen. Shaky handwriting. She knew that she was going to die the following year, before she got the cancer diagnosis after Christmas? She also wrote in the guest book, "I don't want to be a burden on my children and grandchildren. Fortunately I can still walk by myself, with my wheeled walker and a crutch!"

This summer, I have fulfilled her final wish and scattered her ashes on the sea beyond Orrestranda beach "if it's not too much bother for you", as she wrote on a note we found in her writing desk. The one she had inherited from her mother and where she kept all of her papers. The writing desk that my daughter has inherited. When I go to the beach for my morning swim, I think about the ashes. The ashes that are all that are left of her. Roll in her ashes. From ashes to ashes. Mineral matter. Ash is an organic material. Charcoal. Carbon. ^{14}C. Radioactive carbon isotopes. After 5,736 years, half is broken down. To scatter the ashes is a ceremony. A ceremony that she wished for. It symbolises the funeral procession. Parting. What she wrote on one of the post-it notes. *"Servus. Nicht Adé."*[1]

[1] 'Adé' means 'goodbye'. 'Servus' means 'until we meet again'.

The child leaves home. An amputation. The mother's phantom pains. A pathological, dysfunctional loss. Over-emotional consideration, while the young adult child undergoes its megalomaniacal development. Vital and unconscious. A hole in the area of the chest and stomach where the child once inched its way step by step forward into the world. It is to be expected that the fully grown up child – in its injured surprise at the conditions of life and love –will turn to its mother once more. In the meantime, the mother has become so old that the phantom pains have shrivelled up into a careless habit. To repeated affectation. Yes, the old mother gets up again and, with a trace of the greatness of the days of old, directs a cold sneer of welcome towards the middle-aged lost daughters and sons who turn their hearts homewards. Sorry. Too late.

I do not remember who has said this – "The more a person remembers, the closer she is to death." In the light of this hypothesis, her stream of speech, which was directed towards imaginary others this last summer, is perhaps an acute accumulation of dramatic snippets of memory. Fragments that have deposited some especially deep memory traces. Her parting messages indicate that she had an inkling of not having much longer left. Perhaps she was "so difficult" that summer because she, with a mixture of indulgence, contempt, impatience and anxiety, registered our displeasure at something about which she had a kind of certainty.

Like spoilt children, we adults stood open-mouthed, staring affronted at this inconsiderate, egocentric mother of ours. She who had made us into the centrifugal force of her life. Enlivening awakening right before death occurs. Well done, *Mutter*. Give it to them.

I am tidying out the things that Mum left behind in the summer cottage. In drawers and in the loft. I have black bin bags with me that I throw things into. Throw out most of it. Old rugs. Duvets. Bedclothes. Scraps of fabric. Rolls of linoleum. A carrier bag full of stones and chunks of marble that I think Dad was planning to make a mosaic picture out of. A tin of sewing things (I look after that). Old clothes. Also keep completely unused work overalls from the 1970s in bright orange beaver-nylon with yellow reflective crosswise strips. Throw out old tins of paint. A bag of hardened paintbrushes. An old panel heater. Three glass lamp globes. Drawings of Stavanger Cathedral. A reproduction of the Mona Lisa. Beach toys (I look after these). Fishing tackle (that I also take care of). A jacket from Kristiansand Hospital. Information about the old Orre Church and about Kielland's memorial stone. Psalms for a christening. Invitations. Rubbish bags. I take care of three shells. A stone and a marble. A round wooden box with a glass lid. On the inside of the glass, Mum has glued a picture of her mother, Gudrun, sitting on the grass beside the summer cottage. I put the stones, marble, shells, into it. Keep a stone she has written "Ellen" on. A little brass door plaque that says "Ellen Fugelli M. and Ernst L. Mühleisen" on it. She weeded out "Mühleisen" gradually. Dad's name. I look after a pair of waterproof trousers. Three good duvets. Usable bed linen. Bath and kitchen towels. My daughter chooses a matchbox with the logo of the *Spareskillingsbank* in Kristiansand on it because she feels that Mum was so loyal to that bank. Mum and Dad's German motoring atlas. An ashtray. For my youngest daughter, I look after a cigarette case made of crocodile skin.

Vacuum out the narrow loft spaces. Put out rat poison and hammer in some roof nails that are sticking right out. Go down to the beach and have a swim. Walk all the way out into the high breakers. Dive between the waves. My skin opens up to the salt and the memory of the ash particles in the water. Play of colours in the sunlight. Here we meet.

If I am a clever girl and tidy up after me and others clean up after me and others plan visits Christmas celebrations holidays trips birthdays greetings and telephone calls emails and text messages pay the bills organise the repairs funerals maintenance confirmations and cut the grass go on holiday sweep the verandah water the plants take in the bicycles in the autumn the skis out in the winter the cats in at night remember to take vitamins and both stretch and do strengthening exercises if I read books newspapers as well as journals have sex go to exhibitions meet friends and attend to my work every day drink wine sort out photographs if I turn out the light and change the beds go for walks and tidy the cupboards and drawers as well as the lumber room if I also occasionally defrost the freezer polish the windows swim and go to the cinema if I continue steadily with this in the end I die

I look after the paperwork Mum has left behind. Even though I myself have arranged it, I am knocked sideways when the first sum of money from one of her bank accounts is transferred and I receive a letter in the post. Stare at the amount: "43,361 kroner". She always saved. Managed the housekeeping money so carefully so that there would be some left for us. All four. Never spoke for long on the telephone. Bought things mainly in the sales. Darned stockings. Mended clothes. Sewed curtains and bedclothes on an old Singer sewing-machine that Dad added a motor to some time in the 1950s. She subscribed to tax-free savings bonds for all four children. Loaned us money. Gave the grand-children and us money for Christmas and birthday presents. Always asked how we were managing. On minimum pension. Even though she worked for many years as a telephonist. Secretary. Accounts clerk. Now I am dividing up all the money that she has left behind. I wind up her accounts, life insurances and shares. I wipe her out. Cancel her subscriptions. Electricity. Insurance policies. She is deleted from all records. I am zealous in my duty. Want it done as quickly as possible. I can't face any more envelopes with her name on them in my post box. I just stand and stare at the envelope. *I'm getting somewhere now, I'm feeling lighter. I'm coming unstuck from scrapbooks, from albums, from diaries and journals, from space, from time. Only a paragraph left, only a sentence or two, only a whisper. I was born. I was. I.* (Margaret Atwood)

In the end, only the birth and death dates remain: 12.2.1921 – 13.3.2006

12.2.1921
Vennesla
Stavanger
Kragerø
Moss
Oslo
Stavanger
Dale in Hordaland
Stavanger
Grundlsee
Hechingen
München
Kissingen
Aalen
Netztal
Goldach
Mosjøen
Kristiansand
13.3.2006

CONTINUATION

I dream of women. Day and night. Let me lean my head against their breast. Let me drink their milk. The nourishing blood of the umbilical cord. Fill me with sweetness and comfort. Lift me. Promise me that you are with me. Always.

For how long is a person remembered? For as long as someone who knew her, lives. That's not long. Then you have those who left something behind them because they lived public lives. Practised politics. Designed beautiful buildings. Published books. Established operations. Produced works of art. Crimes. Scandals. Knowledge. Technology. Entertainment. War. But as a person in the world, remembered by someone who knew her, has touched her, and lived together with her – all are forgotten just about as fast.

Mum left few traces behind. Not many sources. A diary that she started to write on the 2nd May 1996, when she was 75 years old. A month after Dad's death. The diary is on 142 tightly written pages in Mum's writing that's difficult to read and that became worse eventually as the vigour in her hands deteriorated. She wrote until a few weeks before her death. As far as I know, she hadn't written a diary earlier. I have not read through the whole diary. Read here and there. The notes normally deal with everyday things such as household duties and the weather. Especially the weather. Who was coming, had been on a visit, left. She writes a great deal and clearly about her loneliness. Difficulty with practical tasks. Thoughts about her situation. What she can do to change it. Why she is as she is. She writes often to herself using "you" or addresses herself as "Ellen" and encourages herself to pull herself together. Be better at one thing or another.

6th September, 2003: *Longing? For what? Love? Now you must at the very least manage to cut out smoking, Ellen. Have been out as usual. Will go to bed early. Am so tired. Completely, abnormally tired.*

Among the things she has left behind, there isn't a single letter remaining. Most people leave behind patient records. The demands of the genre in these records are impartiality. Objectivity. Verifiability. Technical terms. The words and descriptions must contain the least possible room for subjective interpretation. A language without metaphors. The neutral speech of truth.

1981: *The patient is a 60 year old woman of slightly below average condition, ambulatory and good general state. Stimulants: 1 and 1/2 pkt tobacco per week.*

1991: *She continues to report a little stabbing sensation in the right half of the thoracic basal plane and a cough, otherwise she has been in good health. She smokes and is extremely ashamed that she hasn't managed to stop.*

1998: *After transfer from the state hospital, she has gradually recovered. She is mostly able to be on her feet and relatively fit.*

2002: *81 year old woman, widow, 4 children. One daughter is a naturopath in London. Has also two children in Oslo and one in Stavanger. She lives alone and manages by herself.*

2002: *The patient has fallen today and sustained a pertrochanteric fracture on the right side.*

2006: *She has therefore a small cell lung cancer with metastases on the liver, consequently widespread disease. After being questioned by her, I have explained that in this case we have no effective treatment.*

2006: *She attended an out-patient appointment today together with her daughter. She lives at home in her own flat, with daily care from the community nurse, when none of her family is staying. She has deteriorated somewhat in the past month, and is clearly an ECOC stage 2 patient. She says that she has reduced appetite, feels nauseous almost every day, and can feel a slight swelling under her right costal arch from time to time. Has no need to talk to a clergyman, but wishes to see the sea from Jæren beach once more before she dies.*

She didn't get to do that – see the sea from Orre-stranda beach at Jæren one last time. Shortly after Mum died, I checked with thumping heart to see if there was a message from her on the telephone answering machine. I realised that I would never again be able to hear her voice. That I don't have a film or a video recording. What would I have done if there was a last message on the answering machine? Listened to it over and over again to hear her voice? Authentic documentation of a life lived. The pitch of her voice. Her accent. The unique voice that spoke to me. There was no message on the answering machine. Now she speaks to me at night. In dreams I always know that she is dead. The first time I dreamed about her, I was overwhelmed at getting to meet her again. I approached her carefully because I was so afraid that she would disappear. I touched her warily and said what was most important of all: "How are you?" and "I love you". She is fine in my dreams. Quiet. Smiling gently. Ignores my anxious questions to a certain degree or replies non-commitally. Reassuring without giving any kind of confirmation.

They might smile, they might not; they might turn away once they know you've seen them. They want you to see them: that's the point. They want you to know they're still around and they can't be forgotten or dismissed.

(Margaret Atwood)

It is getting longer between each dream I have of her. Come to me at night, Mum.

– My hands are shaking so much, she says. Clutching a paintbrush and pressing her lips together. The coffee cup with lukewarm filter coffee. The tobacco pouch and ashtray on the kitchen table. Small tins of paint scattered over the waxed tablecloth. The light comes from the right and makes her thin, still blonde hair, with a touch of permanent wave, shine. – That's why I'm painting in a kind of impressionist style, she giggles, – then the strokes don't have to be so exact. Then she blows her cigarette smoke out to the side and directly into the ray of sunshine.

At the beginning of the 1990s, while Dad was still living, Mum suddenly began to paint and to make things. She went on a watercolour-painting course in Kristiansand. Painted little landscape pictures, fantasy figures. Made small rubbishy sculptures. Decorated old bottles. Constructed wall clocks. She painted on wall-boards that she had cut out. Mounted the workings of a clock and gave these painted wall clocks to her children and grandchildren. Each of my daughters received her own wall clock, with a tiny passport photograph of herself placed among the painted motifs, which were usually flowers, birds or patterns in a collage of foliage. The work took place at the kitchen table. This meant that she had to clear everything away at the end of the activity, so that the table could be used again for meals.

It was quite remarkable that Mum started on these activities, since it was in principle Dad who was "the artist". He had worked in textile design. Was good at drawing and when he retired, he had developed a method of breaking up coloured ceramic tiles and putting them together to make a variety of motifs. He was the one who had the aesthetic judgement in the family. He was also always in despair about Mum's style of interior decoration. She displayed little objects that had sentimental value. She hung up pictures without any higher aesthetic plan. Stones she had collected. Tree roots that resembled a figure. He despised this. Called it *kitsch*. Superficial ornaments. Complained that the flat was crammed with junk. All the same, Mum continued to stage-manage the interior decoration and aesthetics. She also continued to dust the ornaments.

– This is certainly not art, but I think it's fun to potter around with it, she remarked apologetically. But I understood that she was also proud of her works. She said that she, despite wanting to, had never before dared to draw or paint because Dad regarded her work as talentless scribblings. Late rebellion. I too considered this activity as a kind of directionless, amateurish need for self-expression. A bit like how you look on children's drawings. – Lovely, you say. – Wonderful. So clever you are at drawing and painting.

Three of her painted bottles sit at my living room window. They are in fact exquisitely beautiful. Rich in detail in their leafy, partly abstract, partly symbolic, motifs. Delicately matched shades of colour. They are irreplaceable. I wipe the dust off them.

After Dad's death, Mum intensified her painting activities and production of various objects. She began to read books again, after a long break going right back to her youth. She started to write a diary. She wrote her initials in all possible places and recorded on the back of old family photographs who they depicted, when they were born, who their parents were, and so on. She wanted to hold on to some connections. She realised that the memory of some people would disappear with her. She wanted to ensure that some people would perhaps be remembered for a while longer. She wished to produce some signs that showed that she had existed. I read the signs.

The slice of bread tastes good. I like rye bread made from sourdough. Bread like they have in Germany and Austria. To my great pleasure, a few bakeries have started to bake these dark, sourdough-based kinds of bread. I think that it's I who have deserted Mum. Left her in the lurch. I long for mother. Everything becomes as it is and has been. The fear of death slides nicely into position.

I remember the smell in the room those last three days and nights.

Once, you were everything. MOTHER. The mover. Power and mercy in one. Then you became the fragile person. Victim of – sheer chance. Everything so trifling. Specific. The extent of the household budget. Making dinner. Shopping. Paying the electricity bill. And: Is he in a bad mood today? Always with self-doubt. Complaining. Suffering. Lonely. Afraid of the future. I, on the other hand, tracked down grandiose utopias. Systems that proclaimed wholeness, coherence, guarantee of convictions. To protect myself from that helplessness with which you surrounded yourself. The aimless casual nature of coincidences. Because you never saw the connections. Drew conclusions. Completed the actions. In order to draw a brutal line that could register me as something more than your turning away from the world. I was afraid of disappearing. In the claustrophobic protection and meaningfulness of the home. You sat there, without a single book for consolation. It was no use at all.

Wholeness and coherence. Vision. Secure expression of convictions and fellowship. What enlivening, dependency-creating aphrodisiacs I surrounded myself with. How frail you became in comparison, Mum. There you sat at the kitchen table. Make-up. Tobacco. Keys and important memos in the kitchen drawer. All the kitchen drawers down through the years. The kitchen table. Your empire. The kitchen. Your centre of command. No, do you know what! Manifestos instead of shopping lists! 1971: the town square, Mosjøen. Speech on the 1st May. Feminist appeal by the *Kvinnefronten* radicals. Caught sight of you. Somewhere at the very back of the crowd. You looked so small.

1975: Experimental free theatre group. *Thesbiteatret*. Invited to Søgne Folk High School outside Kristiansand. We performed the play *The Brig* by Kenneth Brown. An ultra-realistic stage production of life in an American prison for the navy's own inmates in 1957. Avant-garde political theatre. Cutting edge. We thought. You sat in the audience, Mum.

1977: Friedrichshof, Austria. 120 people with shaved heads, wearing dungarees and sitting in a circle. Someone was playing a piano. Others were beating large drums. I stood right in the middle of the circle of applauding fellow members of the commune and gave an experimental "self-presentation". A mixture of psychodrama and Reich-inspired bio-energetic physical therapy. Improvised theatre. Right at the forefront of the development. We felt. In ecstatic display. Probably. About something or other in my childhood. I think. You were on a visit. You even performed your own version of the self-presentation. In front of all those young shaved skulls in dungarees. You got applause. People were quite impressed that a 56-year-old, bourgeois, timid "core family person"[1] was nevertheless capable

110

of something so radical. Then you travelled home again. To your place. To Dad. The job of being responsible for the accounts in the Roads Department. In Kristiansand. You said you thought we went too far. But the self-presentation was something you yourself plumped for, many years later.

1979: physical, forceful performance about gender, sexuality and feminism at *Club 7* in Oslo. Mum read about it in the newspaper in Kristiansand. The mild-mannered southern Norwegian neighbours were buzzing.

1985: back in Norway after the vain attempt at transformation in what turned out to be the rather closed and hardly liberating experiment in *lebenskunst*. Did you gloat over it? No.

Tøyen Manor House in 2002: The celebration dinner on the day I presented my thesis. All the speeches. You are sitting between my sister and one of my friends. You look old and tired. Think you feel out of place. But you are there.

Then you are no more.

I spread it on so thick. I hammered it in so hard. All those messages of mine.

---

[1]'Core family person' was an expression used in the AAO-commune's categorisation of those who did not live in the commune with its "free sexuality, common ownership, collective responsibility for children and mutual artistic development." AAO was short for the *Aktionsanalytische Organisation*.

Progress report. Leaf through the filofax to find the events I have taken part in. Lecture at the Polytechnic Association on the 7th March, 2006. Six days before she died. My skin tingles. The warmth spreads itself. Heavy lead trickles through all my membranes. My cells are filled with the stuff that death is made of. Again.

Here there are some chairs that Mum left. They were bequeathed by her parents. She herself re-upholstered them. The material is slightly baroque, and I didn't like the chairs when they were in her flat. Should have been leather, as originally, I thought. Now I think they are lovely. Like to sit on them. Look at them. Have them here in my own house. Objects live for so long. Perhaps I shall move into a flat without a single object that links me to the past. Not a photograph. No pictures of my parents. Not a single picture of my children. Not of myself either.

Thinking about you is like reading an old diary.

– Do you recognise your mother in yourself?
Childhood as source.
Mother as the origin.
The mover.
Substance.
I who love my inauthentic self.
My staged persona.
My performative soul.
My strategic desire.
– Do you recognise your mother in yourself?
– Ok. A little, then.

In missing my children, something that comes over me occasionally as insistently and unexpectedly as acute hunger, or an uninvited memory, I recognise my mother's constant and unarticulated longing for us four adult children. She insisted that we were the chosen ones, the most valuable, and for that reason barely acknowledged the people around her, as people it was worthwhile to have dealings with. – I don't feel lonely. I *am* lonely, she stated.

What will I want from my grown-up children? When the children find themselves moving away from me. In just the same way that I once reached in all directions other than those that pointed towards my mother. What should I do there? I possessed her love. There was no expectation connected to a meeting with her. No curiosity. A complete redundancy. As if I knew her. Saw right through her. She never managed to select any places that I wanted to go. She could not conjure up a meaning or fill something with a significance or a puzzle I longed to find out about. She only pointed backwards and inwards towards herself. So it appeared to me.

I could experience conditions of acute claustrophobia by being with her. Through the repetitions of familiar anxieties. Her world was so terrorisingly small and limited. The sliding between control and care. The flat always well-ventilated. It had to do with train times. Meals. Bills. Maintenance. Housing co-operative. Income tax returns. Health worries. Plans for redecoration. Cleaning. Car repairs. Plans about moving house that never came to fruition. Journeys that never took place. Grief over past events that couldn't be changed.

Round in circles. Sometimes I tried to intervene and cheer her up. Appealing, positive suggestions. Creative proposals. Other times in anger. Admonitions. Condescending sarcastic comments. Cold-hearted irony. We siblings all periodically got stuck because of this. We became quite obstinate over all the inward-looking awkwardness. Held tight in impotence over not being able to help her who cried so earnestly for help.

Today her absence has set up a sense of loss. Would I have felt it otherwise? If she had represented something different, perhaps? Awakened a desire for knowledge? Maybe if she too had reached out for something other than me. Than us children. If she had unfolded herself towards something other than what was close at hand. As though all the answers were to be found there.

My children don't know much about me. Don't know many of my friends. Don't know what I read. Don't know what I do every day. What I work at. Who I am with. What I think about. Dream about. Am afraid of. They don't know what I did before they came into the world. They don't know what I am doing after they moved out into the world. I don't know much about my children. Don't know many of their friends. Don't know what they read. Don't know what they do every day. What they work at. Who they are with. What they think about. Dream about. Are afraid of. I don't know what they are doing after they moved out into the world. I don't know much about Mum. Mum didn't know much about me.

Now I know what I was doing when I thought I was reluctantly dusting, taking turns with my sisters to clean in recent years after Mum broke her femur and fretted because of her sense of order and cleanliness. As substitute cleaner, I carried out my tedious obligations with quick, irritated movements. With a suggestion of a martyred expression. What I did not know, was that I was repeatedly touching all those objects that, added together, constituted the sum total of the physical traces of Mum's memory. Thus I archived all of the objects in turn. With the duster as a keyboard. After the container has swallowed everything up, I can therefore, as though in the dark, recreate her universe.

I was possibly expecting a considerate death. Perhaps that she would die easily and meaningfully. Since she had lived so melodramatically and demanded our attention. To the full. Death as personal development. How to die. From the living to the dead. I do not change myself willingly either. In fact only if something pushes down really hard. No reason to die willingly either. Well done, *Mutter*! You resisted. No easy surrender or pathetic resignation here, no. You did it your way. Last show. We stood and gaped. An unforgettable production. The excellent performance of death. Almost reminds a little of my own at the end of the 1970s. Body, breaking of the boundaries of intimacy, the involvement of the public, the thematisation of taboo subjects. The whole thing. Know where I got it from.

What is the difference between thinking about my mother who is alive, but situated in a different place, and thinking about her when she is dead? The concepts eventually stiffen up in the templates because the narrative about her has stopped, because it isn't topped up by new encounters and because I know the story. The ending. As though the ending is an explanation for everything. Cause – effect. Origin – conclusion. Answer. Or I combine elements of the life I think I know, in new ways. Experiments. New hypotheses that turn on connections and make me re-evaluate – everything. My point of view. My poetics. Or does it mean that after I stumble forwards myself, everything changes?

You shone, Mum. Your blonde hair. Your romantic, blue eyes. The pretty, red mouth. Freckles. You smelled so good of a touch of eau de cologne. You were so pretty. So smart and sporty. Classy handbag with a discreet scent of tobacco and a clean handkerchief together with the green purse. You drove a car, used a typewriter and talked to the bank manager. All the other mothers were coarse and dull by comparison. They looked like their own kitchens with a cooped up smell of food. And then you spoke so easily. You just went up to people and talked to them. Just touched them and struck them with your light and laughing voice. People who saw you felt at ease and smiled too. Talked and laughed. You were a bit brazen. You said things right out. You took by surprise. I was proud of you.

I still am.

Until a few years ago, I did not see old people. They were not in any of the places where I was. They never uttered anything that concerned me. If an old person entered my radius, my field of vision, I possibly felt irritation. Perhaps condescension. They were so meaningless. Fussing in front of me in the checkout queue. Slow. Smiled so apologetically. Unpleasantly seeking contact with the pressing, frail physicality they at the same time tried to hide. I saw it well enough. That has changed. When I meet old people nowadays: Sympathy. Recognition. Acknowledgement. I know it well enough. Soon it will be my turn.

I hardly ever experience yearning nowadays. It certainly doesn't quite add up. For example, I still yearn for different places I wish to travel to. Or places I have been earlier, or new places that I imagine. Have read about. Heard of. Latvia. They probably have fine old wooden spa hotels. In Jurmala. Where the power elite in Soviet Russia travelled when they wanted to have a good time. Or a kind of petrol station in the 1950s some place or other in the USA that I have seen in a film. On the whole – when, for instance, I see a landscape in a film or on the television, or a city, I get an impulsive desire to be there. Travel there right now. Feel the wonders of that very place. I sometimes think that I want to become intoxicated. Not in any specific way. Not alcoholic intoxication. That's something that I tolerate only so-so. It is, in all probability, an idea about a condition that I don't really understand, but can long for all the same. Oblivion. Disappear. In a kind of self-sufficient melting together into the world. Don't know if that intoxication exists. Perhaps the old opium dens could offer it. Where a privileged few ventured, lay on chaises-longues, while they were served up a pipe with a suitable dose, conversed with the person in charge, in order to give themselves up to their visions, behind a curtain and under careful watch.

I always dream about all possible shores. Completely wild about beaches. On the other hand it mustn't be too warm. In fact I long unbelievably often to be in a quite specific place in Jæren. That is "the place". Everything is perfectly fitted in my bare feet that have programmed the path down to the shore. The grass when it is cool. Wet. Warmed by the sun. The different smells. The wild flowers before the sand dunes. The stink of dung that is always in the vicinity to differing degrees of intensity. The smell of kelp and seaweed. Wet sand. The light that is part of the sky and changes depending on whether it is morning, midday, night, evening, overcast, windy, rainy, blue skies, summer or winter. Yearn so that it's a bit painful when I am finally there. Because I know that I'll soon be leaving again. I have never been there for long enough. I am quite sure that I'll never get to be there long enough.

I can also yearn, for example, for currywurst. At the moment I'm wondering if I'll manage to find a pair of black trousers that are tight round the ankles. And I'm looking for a pair of cycling trousers. Miss the children now and again. Can also miss others that I like or am fond of. But it's not the same as this unspecified yearning. On the whole, it is true that I hardly ever experience yearning now. In fact I don't miss yearning. It was a load of rubbish. Bloody yearning. Don't understand why people bother.

Mum was constantly yearning. For better weather. The spring. The summer. For Dad to be in a good mood. To be better off financially. For Norway. For a different and better life. For friends. For youth. Always, always, for us. Every single day. In the end she called for her mother.

– You smoked. I don't smoke.
  You drove a car. I don't drive a car.
You didn't wear a cap. I go around in a cap.
You had four children. I had two.
You swam with your head above the water. I swim with
  my head under.
You didn't go to the cinema. I go to the cinema.
You had no lovers. I had many.
You filed your nails. I don't do that.
You ironed handkerchiefs. I have none.
You talked to anyone at all. I don't do that.
You wore a dressing gown. I don't do that.
You painted pictures. I don't do that.
You didn't ride a bike. I do.
You loved me. I love you.

I leaf through one of Mum's old photograph albums bound in stiff covers with an expertly executed pattern of braided straw. A photo of Gudrun. Mum's mother. She is sitting between Mum and Dad's sister. Maria. Summer of 1953. They are sitting outside in the sunshine in front of a window on the wall of the house. Mum must be pregnant with me. Maria unmarried. Working. Living in Germany. Still grieving for her Serbian boyfriend who was killed during the war. Never married. Always exquisitely dressed. Good perfumes. Fashionable leather handbags she carried underneath her arm. Even the oranges and apples in her fruit-bowl were bigger than the ones we had at home. An atmosphere of exclusivity and independence around her. Admired her because she was different from all the other mothers. Housewives. Women in our middle class existence.

Mum and Maria look into the camera. Pretty, young women. The staging of their bodies in front of the camera directed towards them. They are in the moment. Completely self-assured. Gudrun, Mum's mother, was at that time getting treatment for a brain tumour that she would die of a year later. Sitting with both arms on

128

the arm rests. Her hands are hanging heavily, and she casts her eyes down. She will soon be no longer fixed in time. She knows it. She is not smiling self-awarely at the camera. She is not attempting to show herself to advantage. She looks like a hostage between the two young women who direct themselves so vividly towards – us? She knows that she is being documented for the future that will soon come. It is as though she is ashamed – of the young women's frivolity.

Now they are dead too. *In the love that the photograph (certain photographs) arouses, there sounds a different kind of music that has a strangely antiquated name: compassion.* (Roland Barthes) I look at the three women in the photograph with a sympathetic eye. I direct my glance towards the cupboard in the living room. There is a photograph on display there of me together with my two daughters. They are about four and seven years old. The younger is holding onto the handles of a wheelbarrow that is full of vegetables we have harvested at the house of some friends in Vestfold: potatoes, carrots, pumpkins and large squashes. My elder daughter and I are each holding our gigantic squash and look proudly into the camera. My younger daughter looks admiringly at her big sister who is lifting the mega squash up into the air with both arms. A moment's image. We are in a different place now. In time.

There is a photograph of Mum in which she is sitting on the grass beside the wall on the north side of the summer cottage in the evening sunshine. Taken slanted to the side. Is wearing a short-sleeved, white blouse. Open at the neck. And shorts. Her mid-length, blonde hair falls lightly over parts of her face. She is obviously sitting concentrating on her knitting. So young. So full of expectation. Everything that is to come. When I walk past that place, before I round the corner, that photograph strikes me. I remain standing and staring at the spot on the grass beside the house wall. *You sat there then in the bloom of your youth.* Three years ago *you hobbled around here in the decrepitude of your old age.* Here I stand *in the sentimentality of my middle age.*

130

Mum cried out "Mother!" just before she died. She called so heartbreakingly for her mother Gudrun. She who died in 1954. She was then over twenty years younger than Mum was on her deathbed. Good that Gudrun didn't get to see her old, wizened child shout out for her. I feel the same way as you, Gudrun. We who both loved Mum.

March 2009. It is three years since you died. I am sitting again at the dining table in the summer cottage. On the left are the river and the Orre Church. The white-painted farm buildings. Stone dykes. On the other side of the bridge, the little house where Kitty Kielland painted in summer. Right in front, some houses and cottages down beside the sand dunes and the beach. The same as it has always been there. Stone dykes and grass in subdued colours, shades of beige, green, brown, like early in the spring. Make out the white, moving stripe of the surf. Clouds of shifting grey in the big sky. On the horizon it looks as though the sea lights up the sky that is thinned out against the water from below. I sit in the house you loved so much, where some of the original furniture, objects, pictures, have been left in peace. I let my eye glide over the things you had around you, year after year. I look at the landscape you loved to let your eye rest on. Lit up by the sky over Jæren which was the last thing you wanted to see, but didn't manage to. And when I sit outside with my back to the wall of the house and close my eyes, I hear the continual gurgling of the river and the lapwing that has come back after the winter. A faint suggestion of cow dung in the air. It is almost windless. Some way out to sea, where the mouth of the Orre river meets the ocean, your ashes lie.

Work is done. Parents are dead. Children are grown up. Party time.

The demands for future and happiness finally came to an end, Mum. Instead you were able to yield to your disconnected self, your always repressed longing for passivity. You tricked life and us, frantically searching for meaning, together with all the future regimes, by this, your crafty escape route. Death as absolute negativity. A turn-up for the books, where you decidedly give up providing heroic stories of accomplishment and continuity. Not in a direction that gave payoff, oh no. No optimism, either, profit or conclusion in this non-story. This was not therapy. You lay within the short-circuiting of your cells and broken connections like an avant-gardist. Impossible demand that didn't master anything and turned to nothing. Nothing to cross off on the multitude of memos on the kitchen table. So far from mother, wife or woman you became. Denial, freed from the construction of meaning, absolutely without any expectations on the horizon. It was deep down inside, Mum. Now you are free from the sublime. No aesthetics here. No suggestion of harmony or community. Instead, togetherness in shock and catastrophic vulnerability. It was me who lost all control. I will not master your death.

134

I will do it all over again, Mum. When you lie and shout: – "Must, must!" I lift you up carefully. I am not worn out. I have heavenly strength. This is not the fourth night watch. I lift you, and you can sit on the edge of the bed for as long as you like. I support your head, which you can no longer manage to hold up yourself. An arm round your back, because you can't sit on your own. I feed you with a teaspoon of warm honey-water because you can't drink. Everything is accessible when I need it. When you lie on your back and shout: – Mother, Mother! I am there and lift you in my arms and carry you like a child while I sing, *Schlaf, Kindlein, schlaf. Dien Vater hüt die Schaf. Dien Mutter schüttelts Bäumelein. Fällt herab ein Träumelein. Schlaf, Kindlein, schlaf.* Then I lay you down on the newly made bed. Fresh spring air streams through the open window. The room is full of light. Of sunshine. I know everything about dosing with morphine, cramp-relieving medicine and sedative injections. You are not afraid. You feel no pain. It is peaceful. I am with you. Everything is fine. All of the time. When you, for the last time, breathe by fits and starts the no longer life-giving oxygen into your lungs, where the tumour is lying heavy and thinks that it owns the future, then I just take you into my embrace and lift you carefully over.

135